CONTENTS

KT-468-347

YEARS OF TV AND NEWSPAPER REPORTS *have led many people in the west to associate Ethiopia with famine and nothing more. While it is certainly one of the poorest countries in the world, Ethiopia is also one of the oldest, with a rich history, diverse landscapes and a great number of different peoples and cultures.*

HIGHS AND LOWS

Lying in the part of East Africa known as the Horn of Africa, Ethiopia is about five times the size of the UK (or twice the size of Texas in the USA). Stretching from the north to the centre are the Ethiopian Highlands, an area of mountains, grasslands and rivers. Further south, the land becomes much flatter. This region is home to part of East Africa's massive Rift Valley, as well as the Danakil Depression, one of the lowest places on Earth. Here, temperatures can reach as high as 50°C.

ANCIENT TRADITIONS

The contrasting landscapes of Ethiopia are inhabited by people who have adapted to very different habitats and have developed their own unique cultures. There are 80 different ethnic groups in Ethiopia, each with its own language and traditions. Some of these traditions have endured for thousands of years, but in recent decades government resettlement programmes and environmental damage have begun to threaten these ways of life (see pages 8-9 and 12-13).

These maps show Ethiopia's position in the world.

ETHIOPIA

Andrew Campbell

W
FRANKLIN WATTS
LONDON • SYDNEY

This edition 2009

Copyright © 2006, 2009 Franklin Watts

First published in 2006
by Franklin Watts
338 Euston Road
London NW1 3BH

Franklin Watts Australia
Level 17/207 Kent Street
Sydney NSW 2000

A CIP catalogue record for this book is available from the British Library.

Dewey classification number: 916.3

ISBN 978 0 7496 8923 0

Printed in Malaysia

Franklin Watts is a division of Hachette Children's Books,
an Hachette UK company
www.hachette.co.uk

Designer Rita Storey
Editor Sarah Ridley
Art Director Jonathan Hair
Editor-in-Chief John C. Miles
Picture research Diana Morris

Picture credits
Action Press/Rex Features: front cover tr. Matti Bjorkman/Rex Features: front cover b, 27.
Pep Bonet/Panos: 23. Neil Cooper/Still Pictures: 14. Mark Edwards/Still Pictures: 12.
Victor Englebert/Photographers Direct: 5. Indrias Getachew/UNICEF: 25.
Frances Linzee Gordon/Lonely Planet Images: 6. Crispin Hughes/Panos: 19.
Crispin Hughes/Still Pictures: 18. Patricia Jordan/Still Pictures: 8.
Simon Maina/AFP/Getty Images: 16. Knut Mueller/Still Pictures: 20. K. Nomachi/Rex Features: 26.
Picturepoint/Topfoto: 15. Karel Prinsloo/AP/Empics: 11. Reuters/Corbis: 21.
Sipa Press/Rex Features: front cover tl, 13. Sven Torfinn/Panos: 24.
Peter Turnley/Corbis: 1, 9. Petterik Wiggers/Panos: 10.
Richard Young/Rex Features: 17.

*Every attempt has been made to clear copyright. Should there be any
inadvertent omission please apply to the publisher for rectification.*

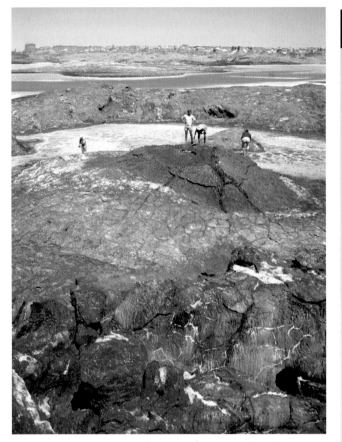

▲ Scientists take an underground water sample in the arid Danakil Depression area of Ethiopia.

BIG ISSUES

Famine is, of course, one reason why Ethiopia is often in the news. The Live8 concerts of 2005 were inspired by the memory of Live Aid in 1985, organised to raise money to relieve the devastating Ethiopian famine of that year. War is another reason why the world's attention has focused on Ethiopia: a war with its neighbour, Eritrea, between 1998 and 2000, still causes problems today (see pages 20-21). Perhaps the biggest reason why Ethiopia hits the headlines is, simply, poverty. Eight out of every ten Ethiopians live on less than $2 a day.

KNOW YOUR FACTS

Here is some information about the countries bordering Ethiopia:

Sudan — Sudan's civil war ended in 2005. But a separate conflict in the western region of Darfur, between Arab military groups and non-Arabs, has created more than 2 million refugees and killed more than 200,000 people.

Uganda — Uganda has won praise for its economic growth and response to HIV/AIDS. In February 2008 the government signed a permanent ceasefire with the Lord's Resistance Army, which was responsible for 20 years of violent conflict.

Kenya — Kenya has been one of Ethiopia's most democratic neighbours, but in early 2008 that meant little. Protestors, who claimed the results of the December 2007 elections were manipulated, killed more than 850.

Somalia — Somalia is one of the most unstable nations in the world. Since 2006 the Islamic Courts Union has controlled parts of the country. Thousands have fled its fundamentalist rule.

Djibouti — Djibouti is a small but important country on the Red Sea coast, lying between Africa and the Middle East. The USA has its only military base in Africa here. In 2008 fighting broke out between Djibouti and Eritrea.

Eritrea — Eritrea achieved independence from Ethiopia in 1993, but then went to war with Yemen and Ethiopia over its borders. The war ended in 2000 but tensions between Eritrea and Ethiopia remain.

ETHIOPIA IS ONE OF THE OLDEST COUNTRIES IN THE WORLD, *with a history stretching back nearly 3,000 years. A major source of pride for Ethiopians is the fact that, while European powers colonised every other part of Africa in the 18th and 19th centuries, Ethiopia remained independent.*

QUEENS AND KINGDOMS

Between 1000 and 400 BCE the first civilisation developed in Ethiopia, influenced by the Sabaean people of southern Arabia. According to the Bible, one of the rulers of Ethiopia, the Queen of Sheba, visited King Solomon of Israel and bore him a son – from whom later Ethiopian emperors claimed descent.

A much more powerful civilisation emerged in the 2nd century CE. This was the kingdom of Aksum, based in present-day northern Ethiopia. Aksum became very wealthy through trade with other countries, but by the 8th century it had lost its power.

CHRISTIANITY AND ISLAM

Ethiopia's rulers and many of its people converted to Christianity in the 4th century CE. After the spread of Islam, four hundred years later, many other countries in Africa followed Arabia by converting to the religion preached by the prophet Muhammad (c.570-632). This left

 This statue in the Ethiopian capital Addis Ababa commemorates the rule of Haile Selassie (1930-74).

Ethiopia cut off from Christianity in Europe and set apart from its Muslim neighbours, who invaded the country between the 13th and 16th centuries to settle and spread their faith.

HAILE SELASSIE

In the 19th and early 20th centuries a series of strong emperors expanded Ethiopia's territory and turned it into a modern, centrally governed country. The last of these rulers was Haile Selassie, who became emperor in 1930 but had to escape to England during Italy's six-year conquest of his country (see panel, right). On his return, he incorporated Eritrea into Ethiopia, made his country a founding member of the United Nations and developed its coffee industry (see pages 18-19). Some people, however, felt Ethiopia could only become truly modern by ending its system of emperor-rule.

DEMOCRACY VIA COMMUNISM

This thinking led to the overthrow of Haile Selassie in 1974, and his murder the next year. The military regime that replaced him, known as the Derg (meaning "committee"), slowly turned Ethiopia into a communist country. The Derg received massive funding from the Soviet Union and transferred the ownership of all land from individuals to the state. But rebellions by different ethnic groups weakened the Derg's control, and in 1991 a new democratic government was formed under the leadership of Meles Zenawi, who became the country's prime minister.

THE ITALIAN OCCUPATION

Ethiopia's first brush with Italy occurred in the late 19th century, when Italy – like France and Britain – was determined to develop an African empire. Italy gained control of the region around Ethiopia, establishing the colony of Eritrea in 1882. By the mid-1930s, Italy – now ruled by the dictator Benito Mussolini – was determined to conquer Ethiopia. Economic developments set in place by Emperor Haile Selassie – such as Ethiopia's growing coffee industry – made the country all the more appealing to the Italian government.

Between late-1935 and mid-1936 the Italians gained control of the country, which joined Eritrea and Italian Somaliland to form Italian East Africa. More than 130,000 Italian workers were shipped over to build roads and houses in Ethiopia – particularly in the capital, Addis Ababa. When Italy joined the Second World War on the side of Hitler's Nazi Germany, Britain recognised Ethiopia as an ally. A joint British-Ethiopian force entered the country in January 1941; in a very short space of time the Italians had surrendered.

THE LARGE NUMBER OF PEOPLE LIVING IN ETHIOPIA – *estimated to be 82 million in 2008 – makes it the third most populated country in Africa, after Nigeria and Egypt. This population is growing all the time: the United Nations believes that it could be as high as 180 million by 2050.*

DIFFERENT CULTURES

Ethiopia is home to many diverse peoples. The biggest ethnic group is the Oromo, who make up around 40 per cent of the population. Oromo have Muslim, Christian or traditional African beliefs, and most work as farmers or cattle breeders. The next largest groups are the Amhara and the Tigray,

who live in the centre and the north and hold Christian beliefs. Other groups include the southern-dwelling Gurage, the Harari – who live in the walled city of Harar in eastern Ethiopia – and the Karo, who paint their bodies in beautiful colours.

NOMADS

Many ethnic groups in Ethiopia continue to live nomadic lifestyles, moving their herds of cattle, sheep, goats or camels from one area of grazing land to another. These peoples include the Somali, the Afar and the Borana. Today, the nomads' centuries-old way of life is threatened as more farmers move onto their traditional lands. The nomads believe that the government should protect their grazing territories, and offer services such as mobile schools for their children. Some politicians, however, regard the nomadic way of life as old-fashioned, and a block to the development of a modern economy.

ETHNIC TENSIONS

Historically, all the different peoples in Ethiopia were able to live quite peacefully together. Starting in the late 20th century, however, ethnic tension has become a sad fact of life. One reason for this is population growth, which has led more and more people to compete with each other for the same amount of land, food and water.

A Karo warrior, balancing a headrest on his shoulder. Karo men decorate themselves using clay, chalk, yellow mineral powder, iron ore and charcoal to imitate the feathers of birds.

New arrivals to regions – either refugees escaping wars in other areas or countries, or people the government has resettled – have added to the unrest. In December 2003, for example, more than 400 people were killed in a single day in Gambela, in western Ethiopia. The fighting was caused by disagreements between the local Anyuak people and the Nuer population, which has risen sharply because of Nuer refugees fleeing the civil war in Sudan.

These Eritreans, displaced by war, have to live in a refugee camp in Ethiopia.

GROUNDS FOR DEBATE

In order to reduce the risk of famine, the Ethiopian government has repeatedly resettled large numbers of people from dry, over-farmed areas to other, more fertile regions. Supporters of this policy argue that by doing this, the resettled people can make a better living from the land. Those against say that the government's actions have disrupted communities and made civil unrest and ethnic tension more likely. What alternative solutions can you think of to moving people between regions?

4 POLITICS

POLITICS IN ETHIOPIA IS VERY COMPLICATED, *with more than a hundred political parties in existence. Most of these parties represent different ethnic groups, and struggle to make their voices heard.*

MELES ZENAWI
The ruling political party, the Ethiopian People's Revolutionary Democratic Front (EPRDF), took power in 1991 and has held on to it ever since, winning three general elections. To many people, its leader and prime minister, Meles Zenawi, is a hero for his role in overthrowing the communist Derg government (see page 7), and he has won praise from Europe and the USA for developing Ethiopia's economy and promoting peace in Sudan and Somalia. Others argue that Zenawi is not the forward-thinking leader he claims to be. They point out that the Ethiopian government still owns all the land in the country, a situation the EPRDF inherited from the Derg and refuses to change.

MIXED RESULTS
The biggest challenge for Ethiopian politics is to ensure that all its ethnic groups are fully represented. The EPRDF is dominated by Tigrayans, who make up between 5 and 10 per cent of the country's population. Other people – particularly the Oromo, the largest ethnic group – think this is unfair. In the 1990s and 2000s many have campaigned for the country to be divided into independent ethnic nations. Such campaigns can involve violence, such as bomb attacks on railway lines and hotels.

ELECTION NEWS – GOOD AND BAD
Land reform and ethnic representation were major issues during the 2005 general elections in Ethiopia. The good news about these elections was the high turnout of voters

This election protest in Addis Ababa in 2005 turned to tragedy when police shot protesters.

Ethiopians queue up to vote in the 2005 elections, in which opposition parties gained popular support.

(about 26 million had the right to vote, making it one of the biggest-ever elections in Africa) and the increasing activity of opposition parties, many of which had refused to take part in the elections of 1995 and 2000 because they mistrusted the government. The EPRDF won the 2005 election, but opposition parties gained more than 30 per cent of the seats in the national parliament.

The bad news was that, as in the 1995 and 2000 elections, many people, including official observers, accused the EPRDF of using threats so that opposition candidates would not stand in the elections and voters would feel scared to vote for any other party. The accusations led to an anti-government protest in Addis Ababa, during which the police shot dead 42 people.

NEARLY EVERY YEAR ETHIOPIA MAKES HEADLINES *around the world because of its food shortages. In 2003 the worst famine loomed in Ethiopia for two decades – more than 13 million people simply did not have enough food to eat. It was only through international aid (see pages 16-17) that a huge disaster was avoided.*

UNRELIABLE NATURE

Some of the factors that lead to famine in Ethiopia, as in other African countries such as Niger and Sudan, are natural ones. Farmers in Ethiopia's dry lowlands

KNOW YOUR FACTS

Ethiopia's 1984-85 famine, in which about 1 million people died, led to a huge international relief effort, the highlight of which was 1985's Live Aid concert. At the time, most people in the west put the famine down to drought; what they did not realise was the role that politics played.
To begin with, Ethiopia's communist government's policies of resettling people into villages and claiming all produce for the state meant that farmers could not grow enough food for themselves and local people. Then, when western governments became aware of the crisis, they were slow to respond – none of them wanted to be seen supporting a communist country. Finally, when food aid did arrive, there were reports that the government used it to feed its army.

irrigate their crops, but rain in this area can be very unreliable. For example, in 2003 both of the country's rainy seasons failed – the *meher*, the heavy summer rains, lasted one month instead of the usual three, while the *berg*, the short spring rains, did not come at all. Besides drought, another problem is locusts, which can eat an entire region's crops.

Dust storms often blow away topsoil, causing devastation.

HUMAN FACTORS

Other problems are human-made. They include poor farming practices, such as cutting down too many trees for firewood and overgrazing land with too many animals. These activities can result in soil erosion, so that even when it does rain the ground is not able to absorb the moisture.

Other causes of famine include government policies such as the state ownership of land, which means individual farmers own small areas of land that produce less than larger areas farmed by the same person. Many people suggest that the biggest cause of all is poverty: farmers are often too poor to buy proper seeds, tools and fertilisers, and people are often too poor to buy food.

MAKING CHANGES

In 2008 Ethiopia faced another food crisis, affecting more than 4 million of its poorest inhabitants. Again, poor rains were one of the causes, but the rising cost of food around the world meant that cereals imported from other countries were much more expensive than in previous years. Some people say that little has improved in Ethiopia since the 1984–85 famine, but others are more positive. The government has made

An image of the 1984 famine. Pictures such as these prompted people around the world to give generously to relieve Ethiopia's distress.

serious efforts to improve Ethiopia's road network, which was one of the worst in Africa. Road-building is vital: in previous famines the roads were so bad or non-existent that food grown in one part of the country could not be transported to another area where it was desperately needed.

NOT ONLY DO MANY ETHIOPIANS SUFFER *from a lack of water, much of the water they do use puts their health at risk. The situation is improving; in 2007, 52 per cent of Ethiopians had access to safe and clean water, up from only 35 per cent in 2005. Yet too many people are still without clean water, as well as adequate sanitation.*

DISEASES

Unclean water and poor waste disposal provide a breeding ground for many diseases. These include malaria, a life-threatening condition carried by mosquitoes (which lay their eggs in water), the skin disease scabies, and trachoma, a type of eye infection.

Diarrhoea is another illness caused by dirty water – for people in the west this is usually just a nuisance, but in poor countries it can be a killer. One report says that 46 per cent of deaths among Ethiopia's under-fives are caused by diarrhoea.

SHORTAGES

One reason for poor levels of hygiene is simply down to water shortages, which force people to drink from still, sometimes stagnant pools, and to be very sparing with their use of water. This can mean, for example, washing clothes less than once a month, even if they are very dirty, and drinking water that may have mud or worms in it. Another reason for poor hygiene is the lack of access to safe toilets. In the capital Addis Ababa, more than a quarter of the 3 million inhabitants use streams running through their housing areas as toilets.

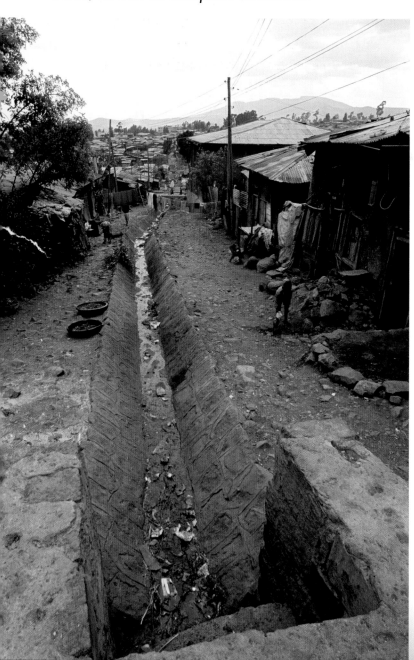

This open sewer runs through a slum area of Addis Ababa.

WORKING TOGETHER

Much needs to be done to improve this situation, and local communities and non-governmental organisations (NGOs) are working hard. The British-based charity WaterAid, for example, brings technical expertise and equipment to help people access fresh water from springs and wells. In the Hitosa region of central Ethiopia, WaterAid has worked with around 60,000 local people to build a massive new water supply scheme.

CLEANING UP

In the Tekle Haymonot district of Addis Ababa, locals are working to improve their sanitation levels in a different way. Each morning, people collect rubbish from houses in the district – rubbish which otherwise would have been left in the streets. Each household pays a small charge for this service, and is responsible for keeping the area outside its front door clean. The result has been a big improvement in the health of residents.

KNOW YOUR FACTS

Water shortages mean that Ethiopians, usually women, often have to walk long distances to fetch and carry supplies. Birkenesh Belete explains what life was like in her home of Boloso Sore, in southwest Ethiopia, before the charity Oxfam installed a water pump in her village: "We couldn't go twice to the river to fill and carry our pots as we had to leave at 4 am and didn't get back until 11 am. Then we had a lot of work to do. We had stomach problems, and our backs ached. We had problems in the pelvic area. Our legs ached from walking. We got headaches from getting up early and not getting enough sleep."

This young girl walks many kilometres to fetch fresh water in the jar on her back.

DEVELOPMENT MEANS ANY ASSISTANCE *from rich countries that helps poor nations to become wealthier, more stable and ultimately more able to cope without outside support. Development is a crucial issue in Ethiopia, where life expectancy is on average 54 years (compared to 79 years in France and the UK, and 80 in Australia).*

AID

In 2005 the Make Poverty History campaign, which brought together many international charities and NGOs, addressed the three types of development support that countries like Ethiopia need: aid, debt relief and trade justice. Aid comes in many different forms. One form is emergency aid, which governments and NGOs send in response to crises such as Ethiopia's 2003 famine. This assistance is vital, but often takes months to reach the neediest places. Many argue that long-term aid, such as providing farmers with better seeds and tools, is more beneficial.

DEBT RELIEF

Debt relief is another way to help Ethiopia build its economy. Like other African countries, Ethiopia has borrowed a lot of money from western banks and governments since the 1970s.

 Road-building, shown here, is vital to Ethiopia's development.

GROUNDS FOR DEBATE

Have campaigns such as Make Poverty History achieved anything in Ethiopia? Yes, say its supporters. Life expectancy is up and childhood deaths are down, Ethiopia's economy grew by 10 per cent each year between 2005 and 2008, and there are now 14 million Ethiopian children in primary school. Do you think campaigns like Make Poverty History make a difference?

Because interest rates have risen very quickly during this period, much of the money Ethiopia paid back simply covered this increase and did not reduce the original debt. In 2002, for example, Ethiopia spent more money on its debts than on healthcare or education. In July 2005, however, leaders of the world's eight richest countries – the G8 – met in Scotland and agreed to cancel the debts of 18 of the world's poorest nations, including Ethiopia. This is a huge step forward, but some people are worried that rich countries will still recover the money owed to them by reducing the amount of aid they give.

TRADE JUSTICE

Many Make Poverty History campaigners, along with many Ethiopians, argue that there is only one way to really help poor countries stand on their own two feet –

by making trade fair. This means that western governments should stop the subsidies (payments) they give their own farmers to produce more food than is needed – a system which was first set up in Europe after the Second World War to prevent a repeat of wartime food shortages. It also means that western countries should remove the barriers that prevent producers in poor countries from selling their goods to richer nations.

 Bob Geldof (left), with Paul McCartney (right), organised the Live8 concerts in 2005 to focus the world's attention on poverty and debt relief.

COFFEE GROWING IS ETHIOPIA'S MOST IMPORTANT INDUSTRY *and source of income. Around 15 million Ethiopians are involved in the coffee trade, either as farmers or processors, and about 35 per cent of the money Ethiopia earns from selling goods to other countries comes from coffee.*

COFFEE TALES

Ethiopia is the birthplace of coffee. According to Ethiopian history, coffee was discovered in about 1000 CE, when a goat herder in Choche, in western Ethiopia, noticed that his goats made a lot of noise and refused to sleep after eating some strange berries. The goat herder tried the berries himself, and found that he was no longer tired. Today, coffee plays a large part in Ethiopian culture. Visitors to a

▼ Coffee cherries are the ripe fruit of the coffee bush.

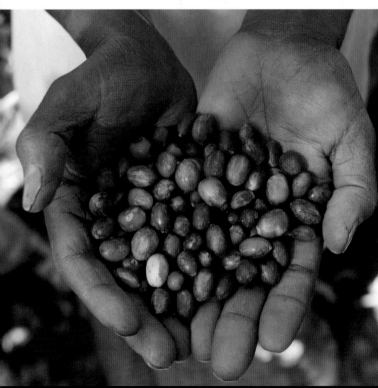

home will often wait while the host roasts the coffee beans, brews and serves the coffee in tiny cups. It is traditional for a guest to be served at least three cups.

PRICE SLUMP

Since the late 1990s, Ethiopia's coffee farmers have faced a very difficult situation. Brazil and Vietnam both increased the amount of cheap coffee they produced, with the result that there

KNOW YOUR FACTS

Coffee is the second most valuable product in the world, after oil; people around the world drink about 2.5 billion cups of coffee every day. The two most widely grown varieties of coffee are arabica, which is mild in flavour, and the stronger-tasting robusta. Arabica is the main coffee grown in Ethiopia.

After the coffee cherries are harvested, they go to warehouses for sorting, pulping, fermenting, washing and drying. The coffee beans are then bagged and shipped to western countries for roasting and blending. Ethiopian farmers receive, on average, 2 per cent of the price we pay for a jar or cup of coffee. The roaster (usually a big multinational company) receives an average of 64 per cent, and the retailer 25 per cent.

Farmers harvest the coffee cherries between late September and December.

was simply too much coffee on the world market, and prices collapsed. In the mid-1990s, farmers in Choche, for example, sold their coffee for the equivalent of about £1.95 per kilogramme. By the early 2000s, this had dropped to 20 pence or less for the same amount. Many farmers could not afford adequate food, or to send their children to school.

TOO MUCH CHAT

Many farmers began to replace their coffee crops with chat, a plant whose leaves are chewed or boiled as a mild drug. Chat is popular in Ethiopia, so at least farmers can earn money this way. However, growing it involves clearing the acacias and other trees under which coffee bushes grow, which can damage the local environment.

COFFEE CO-OPERATIVES

Another way coffee farmers can protect their interests is to join a coffee co-operative. Many farmers sell their beans to traders, who sell them to exporters who, in turn, sell them to foreign buyers – from Nestlé to Starbucks. Co-operatives, on the other hand, buy from the farmer and sell directly to international buyers, including Fairtrade coffee companies, which pay farmers more and so charge customers more in return. Co-operatives share any profits they make with farmers; they also help them transport and store their beans, offer loans for new equipment and educate farmers about the world coffee market and changing international tastes.

FROM 1998 UNTIL 2000 A WAR BETWEEN ETHIOPIA *and its northern neighbour Eritrea killed as many as 75,000 people and forced more than 350,000 to flee their homes. Today, the aftermath of the war continues to affect many people on both sides.*

FROM FRIENDS TO ENEMIES

Eritrea became part of Ethiopia in 1962, but, following the overthrow of Ethiopia's communist government in 1991, became independent again in 1993. Relations between the two countries were, at this time, good: Ethiopia's prime minister Meles Zenawi and Eritrea's president Isaias Afewerki were friends who had fought alongside each other against the communist regime. In May 1998, however, Eritrea moved soldiers into the region of Badme on Ethiopia's north-western border. When Eritrea refused to withdraw, Ethiopia declared war.

WAR AND UNEASY PEACE

Both sides assembled around 300,000 soldiers along the border, while their air forces bombed each other's airports and towns. Ethiopia forced thousands of Eritreans living inside its border north into Eritrea; Eritrea responded by expelling thousands of Ethiopians. The violence and refugee crisis continued until June 2000, when both governments called a ceasefire. They agreed to set up an independent boundary commission, made up of lawyers who would decide how the border between the two nations should be fixed. In 2003 the commission decided on a new border – changes included giving Badme to Eritrea. The Ethiopian government has refused to accept this decision, and tension between both sides rumbles on.

THE HUMAN COST

People on both sides of the Ethiopian-Eritrean border continue to suffer because of the war. Many still live in refugee camps and others are at risk from landmines, planted along the border during the war. Between 1998 and 2003, 550 landmine explosions injured or killed civilians – and these were just the incidents that were reported.

Starving Eritrean refugees await grain distribution from the World Food Program.

The costs of war have been huge for both countries. Ethiopia spent hundreds of millions of dollars on the conflict, which also caused many foreign businesses to stop investing in the country. All this is money that Ethiopia desperately needs. Another effect of the war has been to reduce Ethiopia's access to the sea. Previously it relied on Eritrea's ports of Assab and Massawi to send and receive goods by ship; now businesses have to use the port of Djibouti, a small country to the northeast.

 An Eritrean soldier keeps guard near the border with Ethiopia.

KNOW YOUR FACTS

The dispute over the 900-km border between Ethiopia and Eritrea is a matter of national pride. Eritrea argues that the border should reflect the one fixed by Italy in 1902 while Ethiopia wants the border to be where it was before Eritrea's invasion in 1998. During the 1980s, Ethiopian Tigrayans, rebelling against their communist government, expanded their control into Eritrean territory. Since they then became the dominant group in Ethiopia's new government, this territory has remained part of Ethiopia.

LIKE MANY OTHER POOR COUNTRIES – *especially in Africa – Ethiopia has a major HIV/AIDS problem. Just under a million Ethiopians are believed to be HIV positive, and while infection levels are slowly falling, many people still do not know enough about the risks and prevention of this killer disease.*

YOUTH AT RISK

There are many reasons why HIV infections occur in Ethiopia, from cultural barriers about condom use to a lack of information about how to avoid infection. According to a United Nations survey in 2005, only 21 per cent of young women and 33 per cent of young men aged between 15 and 24 years had a "comprehensive knowledge" about HIV and AIDS.

GET THE MESSAGE

Education is therefore crucial in spreading awareness about HIV and AIDS to ordinary Ethiopians. Peer education – young people teaching other young people – is a powerful way to get the message across, and is actively encouraged by the government. One peer education group is the Tabor-Wegagen Anti-AIDS Association, which was set up by a group of young people. Members of the association teach teenagers about HIV and AIDS for a period of two months. They also write and perform plays on AIDS topics.

AIDS AND CHILDREN

There are as many as 1.2 million AIDS orphans in Ethiopia – children whose parents have died from the disease. On 25 October 2005, Richard Mabala, the head of UNICEF's Youth, Protection and HIV/AIDS programme in Ethiopia, spoke about their situation:

"The Global Campaign being launched today talks about children as the Missing Face of AIDS. Maybe we could talk about the missing faces, or even the invisible faces. Instead the faces have been turned into staggering statistics, huge numbers that we throw around in our speeches, xxx infected every minute, yyy orphans, zzz numbers of children needing treatment, etc. And as we stand and pronounce the statistics, they continue to get bigger so that our next speech will have to revise the statistics up once again. And because the statistics are so big, just like a hurricane Katrina or a tsunami, or an earthquake, they can actually disempower us as we are overcome by a sense of helplessness. How can we ever hope to deal with such a situation? Where do we start? How can we find the resources? And yet each one of these statistics dreams, just like you and I dream. In our case, our dreams inspire us to action."

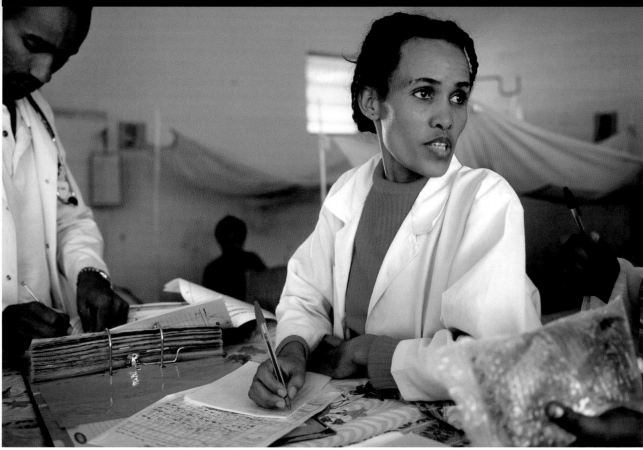

▲ Workers distribute ARVs at a hospital in Humera, near the Eritrean border.

WHAT PRICE A LIFE?

The real issue for those who have HIV or AIDS, however, is gaining access to drugs called anti-retrovirals (ARVs). ARVs can help HIV-infected people to live healthy lives, and have led to a reduction in AIDS-related deaths in the west. But most people in Ethiopia, like the rest of Africa, cannot afford the cost of ARV treatment. In 2007, according to Ethiopian estimates, nearly 260,000 Ethiopians needed ARVs – but many fewer were actually receiving drugs. The World Health Organization has led a campaign to massively increase the number of people on ARVs in Ethiopia, but progress has been slow.

GROUNDS FOR DEBATE

One reason why ARVs are not as widely available as they could be is that drug companies refuse to allow "generic" drug manufacturers to make cheap copies of their medicines. The drug companies say that, in a free market, the right to profit from the sale of their product should be protected. Opponents say that the drug companies should be forced to allow cheap copies to be made to deal with the HIV/AIDS humanitarian emergency. What do you think?

IT IS NOT EASY GROWING UP IN ETHIOPIA. *As many as half a million children die each year from diseases and malnutrition. For those that survive, childhood can be cut short by early marriage or the need to work to support families.*

EARLY MARRIAGE

Getting married at an early age – as young as eight or nine – is common in Ethiopia. According to government figures, 57 per cent of girls marry before the age of 18, while in some regions (such as Amhara and Tigray) this can be around 80 per cent. Arranged marriages are a major way of securing alliances between families. In addition, because life expectancy is low, parents have an extra desire to see their children married and settled as quickly as possible – unmarried girls and women risk being seen as outcasts in Ethiopian society.

CHILD LABOUR

Boys can get married at an early age too, although this is more common for girls, who as wives are expected to cook, clean, collect firewood and water and help with farming tasks. Boys will often assist their fathers by tending cattle, planting seeds, looking after crops and helping to harvest them. This pattern of

▼ Children and teenagers gather outside a school in Tsiska, near Lalibela.

family responsibility and farming duties is repeated across Ethiopia, where the vast majority of people live in the countryside.

SCHOOL PROBLEMS

Although around seven out of every ten Ethiopian children go to primary school, many drop out or do not go on to secondary school. Early marriage and child labour partly explain this situation; other reasons can be that schools are few and far between – children may have to walk long distances to get to school and, when they get there, classes can number more than 100 children. Another factor is poverty: parents have no money for school uniforms or books, and need their children to stay at home and work.

CHANGING ATTITUDES

Many people believe that changing parents' attitudes will help children have more access to education. Many Ethiopians have traditionally placed little value on girls' schooling, so teachers persuade parents that everyone has a right to education, and that early marriage can harm young people's development.

One positive example has been set by Samia Sadik, a student from Dire Dawa in eastern Ethiopia. Samia refused to accept her parents' wishes and get married, a decision her schoolteachers supported her in making. Samia has now completed her secondary schooling, and hopes to become a doctor.

Samia Sadik, now training to become a doctor.

EDUCATION

Ethiopia's world champion runner, Berhane Adere, is a campaigner for increasing children's access to sports and education in her home country: "Education is important for every child, because education is something that is above everything else. Being educated means having knowledge. Being educated allows you to eat, drink and clothe yourself. You are able to understand things if you are educated. The country can grow if there is education. I believe that everyone needs to be educated."

AS ETHIOPIA'S GOVERNMENT AND PEOPLE LOOK TO THE FUTURE, *the need to develop the country's economy – to cope with a growing population, poverty, drought and health problems – becomes more urgent. Tourism is seen by many as a possible solution, which could earn Ethiopia millions of vital dollars.*

PLACES TO VISIT

Ethiopia certainly has lots of tourist potential. Attractions include Addis Ababa's open-air market, the Merkato, said to be the biggest in Africa, the stunning Simien mountains in the north and the town of Lalibela, with its 11th- and 12th-century churches carved out of volcanic rock. Ethiopians are world-famous for their friendliness, and their customs and celebrations are fascinating to watch and take part in. The country is also home to a rich plant and animal life, including 28 mammal species found nowhere else on Earth, such as the mountain nyala (a type of antelope) and the Ethiopian wolf.

PROBLEMS TO FIX?

Some people argue that Ethiopia has a long way to go before it can seriously offer itself as a tourist destination on a large scale. Its road network is still very

Traditional dances – such as this one performed by the Hama people – attract tourists.

The recent success of Ethiopia's middle-distance runners is helping to change attitudes to the country around the world.

limited, for example, and outside Addis Ababa there are few hotels that can meet the expectations of wealthy western visitors. Others point out that roads and hotels are being built. A bigger issue might well be the country's image: many people in the west – unfairly – see Ethiopia in terms of famine and poverty, and not as a holiday destination.

OTHER THINGS FIRST

Many people think that Ethiopia needs to concentrate on other industries before tourism. Agriculture is by far the country's biggest earner, and for things to improve farmers need to diversify their crops away from coffee and grow more grains, sugar, fruit and vegetables. One "growth" industry in Ethiopia is flower farming, which employs around 80,000 people. Ethiopia now rivals its neighbour Kenya as a major exporter of flowers, in particular roses, which are sold in countries such as the UK and Germany.

1000–400 BCE: First civilisation develops in Ethiopia.

2ND CENTURY CE: Kingdom of Aksum established in present-day northern Ethiopia.

4TH CENTURY: Introduction of Christianity to Ethiopia from Egypt.

8TH CENTURY: Aksumite power collapses.

1530–31: Muslim forces conquer much of Ethiopia.

1818: The military leader Lij Kassa begins building up power in previously separate Ethiopian regions.

1855: Lij Kassa becomes Emperor Tewodros II.

1889: Emperor Menelik II, king of Shoa in central Ethiopia, takes the throne.

1895: Italy invades Ethiopia. The Italians are defeated the next year but retain control of Eritrea.

1916: Menelik II's daughter, Zawditu, comes to the throne but rules through her cousin, Ras Tafari Makonnen.

1930: Ras Tafari is crowned Emperor Haile Selassie.

1935: Italy invades Ethiopia for the second time. The Italians rule Ethiopia and Eritrea until 1941, when British and Ethiopian soldiers force them out.

1962: Haile Selassie makes Eritrea part of Ethiopia.

1972–74: Around 200,000 people die because of famine in north-central Ethiopia.

1974: A military coup led by the Derg (committee) forces Haile Selassie from power.

1977: Colonel Mengistu Haile Mariam becomes Ethiopia's leader.

1977–78: Mengistu orders a campaign of intimidation against opponents of the Derg – thousands of people are killed.

1984–85: Famine in Ethiopia kills up to 1 million people.

1986: The country's first AIDS cases are reported.

1989: The Tigrayan People's Liberation Front joins forces with other ethnic opposition movements to the Derg to become the Ethiopian People's Revolutionary Democratic Front (EPRDF).

1991: EPRDF forces expel Mengistu from the country and take over power.

1993: Eritrea becomes independent from Ethiopia.

1994: A new constitution divides the country into nine regional states and two self-governing cities, Addis Ababa and Dire Dawa.

1995: Ethiopia holds its first democratic elections; Meles Zenawi, the EPRDF leader, becomes prime minister.

1998: Start of the two-year Ethiopia-Eritrea war.

2000: The Ethiopian and Eritrean governments sign a peace agreement in Algeria.

2000: Haile Selassie, murdered by the Derg in 1975, is finally buried in Addis Ababa's Trinity Cathedral.

2000: Ethiopia's coffee industry crashes.

2003: An independent boundary commission decides on the new border between Ethiopia and Eritrea. Ethiopia refuses to accept the decision.

2004: The government begins a resettlement programme to move more than 2 million from drought-affected regions.

2005: The third general election since the overthrow of the Derg is held. There are claims of electoral fraud, and police shoot dead 42 protestors.

2005: G8 leaders agree to cancel all Ethiopia's outstanding debts.

2007: Human rights groups accuse the Ethiopian government of war crimes in its military crackdown on an independence campaign in the region of Ogaden.

2007: Ethiopia celebrates the start of its new millennium (in accordance with the calendar of the Coptic Orthodox Church, the main Christian Church in Ethiopia).

BASIC FACTS

LOCATION: East Africa.

TOTAL LAND AREA: 1,133,380 sq km.

POPULATION: 82,544,840 (2008 estimate). Population growth rate: 2.36 per cent (2005 estimate).

MAJOR ETHNIC GROUPS: Oromo, Amhara, Tigray, Sidamo, Shankella, Somali, Afar, Gurange.

EMPLOYMENT AND INDUSTRIES: agriculture (85 per cent of population), mining, chemicals.

HIGHEST MOUNTAIN: Ras Dashen (4,620 metres), the 4th highest in Africa.

MAJOR RIVERS: the Blue Nile, the Awash, the Omo, the Wabe Shebele.

AIDS (Acquired Immune Deficiency Syndrome)   A collection of infections and cancers that people with HIV can develop.

Anti-retrovirals (ARVs)   Drugs that act against the HIV virus, by stopping it making copies of itself inside white blood cells.

Civil war   A war between rival groups within a country. African history since the late 20th century is full of civil wars – Ethiopia is no exception.

Communism   A political and economic system in which the state, or total community under a government, owns all the property. Individuals are provided with work, food and housing.

Ethnic group   A group of people that are bound together by their race, language, traditions or nation.

Ethnic representation   Standing up for the rights of individual ethnic groups. Many people think there should be more ethnic representation in Ethiopia since the government is dominated by one ethnic group.

Famine   An extreme and long-lasting food shortage, leading to malnutrition (a condition caused by eating poor or inadequate food), starvation and possibly death.

HIV (Human Immunodeficiency Virus)   The virus that causes people to develop AIDS. Once someone is infected with HIV it stays with them for life.

Irrigation   An artificial system that channels water through farmland to help farmers grow crops. Very little of Ethiopia's farmlands are currently irrigated.

Landmine   An explosive device buried in the ground. During war, soldiers bury landmines so that enemy troops or vehicles will tread on them, causing an explosion. After wars, however, unexploded landmines remain in the ground, and can be set off by civilians – often children – and animals.

Land reform   Efforts to change the way land is owned. In Ethiopia, many demand land reform to end the state, or national, ownership of land, which dates back to the communist period.

Life expectancy   The average age that a person can expect to live to. Life expectancy is much lower in Ethiopia than in western countries.

Nomad   Someone with no fixed home who moves about a particular region or territory, usually with animals.

Non-governmental organisations (NGOs)   Independent, not-for-profit organisations that campaign, provide a service or help people.

Refugees   People who are forced to leave their homes because of war or political upheaval. Many escape to other countries where they apply for asylum (permission to remain).

Resettlement programme   A government scheme to move large numbers of people from one region to another – in Ethiopia's case away from drought-ridden or over-farmed areas to more fertile ones.

Soil erosion   When soil that is not protected by plants blows away in the wind or is washed away by heavy rains. Cutting down trees and overgrazing are two causes of soil erosion.

Soviet Union   Communist empire that consisted of Russia and much of eastern Europe and central Asia. It lasted from 1917 to 1991.

USEFUL WEBSITES

http://www.addisfortune.com
The online version of Ethiopia's English-language newspaper.

http://www.ena.gov.et
The Ethiopian News Agency – the official news site of the Ethiopian government.

http://www.ethiographer.com
An online gallery of photographs from around Ethiopia.

http://www.ethiopians.com
Lots of information about Ethiopia.

United Nations   The international organisation established in 1945 to promote peace and co-operation between countries.

UNICEF (United Nations Children's Fund)   An agency of the United Nations that runs development programmes for children in developing countries.

World Health Organization   An agency of the United Nations, set up in 1948 to promote health and tackle disease around the world.

http://www.oxfam.org.uk/oxfam_in_action/where_we_work/ethiopia.html
Read about the development work Oxfam undertakes in Ethiopia.

http://www.wateraid.org.uk
Find out about this charity which helps countries gain more access to clean water.

http://www.unaids.org
The website of UNAIDS features country profiles of the impact of HIV and AIDS.

http://www.unicef.org/ethiopia
The website of UNICEF in Ethiopia – learn about its role in helping to deal with poverty, health and education issues.

Note to parents and teachers:
Every effort has been made by the Publishers to ensure that the websites in this book are suitable for children, that they are of the highest educational value, and that they contain no inappropriate or offensive material. However, because of the nature of the Internet, it is impossible to guarantee that the contents of these sites will not be altered. We strongly advise that Internet access is supervised by a responsible adult.